# REVIEW OF THE POSSE COMITATUS ACT AFTER HURRICANE KATRINA

The Posse Comitatus Act of 1878 (PCA) and as amended restricts the use of the Army or the Air Force for law enforcement purposes.[1] The PCA limits the ability of the military to directly and rapidly respond to domestic events such as natural disasters, civil unrest, and acts of terrorism.[2] Hurricane Katrina and the events of September 11, 2001, combined with the potential for use of a weapon of mass destruction (WMD) in a domestic terrorist event have brought the PCA into the spotlight for review. Immediately after Hurricane Katrina President Bush promoted the idea of the military playing a primary role in responding to future disasters or national crises and for Congress to consider review of the law.[3] This paper provides background on the issue of the use of the military for law enforcement and makes the case that policy and not necessarily statutory guidance drives the use of the military in the domestic venue for rapidly responding to a wide range of crises.

In 1932, Major George S. Patton, Jr., Cavalry, opined in writing about using federal troops in domestic disturbances:

> Due to the combined effect of ignorance and careless diction, there is widespread misunderstanding of the principle terms used in connection with the enforcement of law by military means.[4]

Not much has changed since then and especially so when it comes to the PCA. Patton said, "To be a successful soldier you must know history."[5] Therefore the history of the PCA from its roots to its branches requires exploration to combat the ignorance and misunderstanding of the PCA and use of the military for law enforcement.

## Foundation of Law in the United States of America

From the First Continental Congress in 1774 to the adoption of the Bill of Rights in 1791, the founding fathers carefully crafted the foundation of the United States of America.[6] The Declaration of Independence in 1776 established the United States of America as free and independent states from British rule.[7] The Articles of Confederation, developed immediately after the Declaration of Independence, submitted to the states in 1777, and finally ratified in 1781 legalized the ad hoc government with Congress at its center.[8] The financial failure of the Confederation government in practice led to the Constitutional Convention in 1787.[9] Over a period of four months in 1787, the Constitutional Convention produced the preamble and seven articles establishing the Constitution of the United States of America, ratified in 1788, forming the government with legislative, executive, and judicial branches.[10] The first ten amendments to the Constitution of the United States, which became universally known as the Bill of Rights, were immediately proposed in 1789, and ratified in 1791, as a promised requirement for the ratification of the Constitution.[11] The durability of the Constitution is made obvious in the context of history as it was conceived in an eighteenth-century agrarian republic and endures in an evolving twentieth-century urban industrial economy that is transforming through globalization into the twenty-first century.[12] Consistent throughout the foundation of law in the United States of America is the relationship between the military and the public.

The American public has a longstanding tradition of mistrust of standing armies seeing them as instruments of oppression and tyranny.[13] The Boston massacre of 1770 represents a pivotal point in this mistrust when the British Army, sent to Boston to act as a police force, fired on rioters clearly in violation of the due process principles outlined in colonial charters.[14] The Declaration of Independence that ultimately followed decried the use of armies and attacked keeping a standing army in peace, the military's independence from civilian control, and the quartering of troops among the population.[15] The Articles of Confederation limited the role of the military by restricting the raising of armies and the maintenance of naval vessels.[16] The Constitution mandated civilian control by designating the President as Commander-in-Chief of the military, and while allowing for a standing army and maintenance of a navy, it restricted military appropriation to two years.[17] The Bill of Rights prohibited the quartering of soldiers in private homes and ensured the states of a militia as a counterbalance to a standing army.[18] Additional provisions of the Bill of Rights, including the First and Fourth Amendments, prevent a reoccurrence of the types of abuses committed by the British Army in colonial times by allowing free speech and press, peaceful assembly, the petition of grievances, and relief from unreasonable searches and seizures.[19] The foundation of law in the United States of America is consistent in ensuring that the federal government does not exert undue influence directly on the public through the military.

Basis for the Posse Comitatus Act

In spite of all of the provisions provided by our founding fathers to control the organization and use of the military, Congress found it necessary after the 1861-1865 Civil War to restrict the use of the military as posse comitatus with passage of the PCA in 1878.[20] Posse comitatus is the English common law doctrine of the power of the county, or the citizens who may be summoned by the sheriff to assist the authorities in suppressing a riot, or executing any legal precept which is forcibly opposed.[21] Prior to the PCA, the U.S. military's involvement in law enforcement was neither illegal, nor uncommon.[22] In 1794, President Washington used the military to put down the Whiskey Rebellion in Western Pennsylvania.[23]

The Judicial Act of 1798 allowed any U.S. federal marshal to create a posse comitatus using the military. [24] This was reinforced in 1854 by Caleb Cushing, the U.S. Attorney General under President Franklin Pierce, with a legal ruling affirming the posse comitatus doctrine in response to an incident involving a U.S. federal marshal using the assistance of state militia in the enforcement of the Fugitive Slave Act of 1850.[25] That ruling subsequently became known as the Cushing Doctrine and the basis for further use of the military as posse comitatus.[26] The Cushing Doctrine arose out of the need for a ruling on the legality of the commission of an act. That ruling established policy, but not necessarily law.

The increased use of the military in law enforcement during the 1800's in administration of the new territories culminated in direct military involvement in the reconstruction of the ex-Confederate States of the South after the Civil War.[27] During the Presidential Election of 1876, a Republican President Grant sent federal troops to polling places in the South to ensure the rights of black citizens to vote.[28] Southern Democrats perceived the presence of federal troops as allowing the stealing of a close election by the Republican candidate, Rutherford B. Hayes, based upon the votes from three southern states.[29] Political battles resolving the close presidential election led to the effective withdrawal of federal troops from the South in early 1877.[30] The Democratic controlled House of Representatives wanted to ensure the South remained free of federal interference after the withdrawal of federal troops, but failed to attain agreement from the Republican controlled Senate on the 1877 Army appropriation bill passed in the House of Representatives, which expressly prohibited use of the Army to shore up Republican state governments in the South.[31] Subsequently, the Southern Democrats allied with the Northern Democrats, who opposed the use of the Army to crush the railroad union riots of 1877, to propose an amendment to the 1878 Army appropriation bill placing restrictions on the use of the military as posse comitatus.[32] After extensive negotiations in conference, the amendment finally passed both the House of Representatives and the Senate, and became known as the Posse Comitatus Act (PCA). [33]

The PCA is a criminal statute codified in Title 18, Section 1385 of the United States Code (U.S.C.) that restricts any direct involvement of the military in enforcing civilian laws except when expressly authorized:

> Title 18 U.S. Code § 1385. Use of Army and Air Force as posse comitatus. Whoever, except in cases and under circumstances expressly authorized by the Constitution or Act of Congress, willfully uses any part of the Army or the Air Force as a posse comitatus or otherwise to execute the laws shall be fined under this title or imprisoned not more than two years, or both. [34]

The PCA is law, enacted by Congress, overturning the Cushing Doctrine that allowed a U.S. federal marshal to use the military as posse comitatus. The PCA does not completely prohibit, nor prevent the use of the military from performing law enforcement. The PCA requires that the use of the military for law enforcement is at the direction of Congress or the President on a constitutional or statutory basis. The Army welcomed the PCA, as the use of soldiers as a posse comitatus typically placed them under the control of local authorities who had an interest in the issue that created the unrest.[35] Many officers viewed the use of the military as a posse comitatus as corrupting and politicizing the military institution.[36]

Shortly after signing the PCA on 18 June 1878, President Hayes successfully deployed troops to the New Mexico Territory to enforce the law, affirming the only effective limit of the PCA was Presidential involvement in using the military for law enforcement.[37] An 1882 Senate Judiciary Committee report confirmed that the President could use troops for law enforcement provided that military officers retained command, and that the issue addressed by the PCA was a U.S. federal marshal's ability to use the Army as a posse comitatus.[38] From 1877 to 1945 the Army was effectively involved in 125 law enforcement interventions, proving that the PCA does not prohibit, nor prevent the use of the military for law enforcement.[39]

Application of the Posse Comitatus Act

The PCA explicitly restricts the Army, that standing army of such great concern in the development of the Constitution. Initially the PCA only applied to the Army and was extended to the Air Force under the National Security Act of 1947.[40] The Navy and the Marines are not restricted by the PCA, but the Department of Defense (DoD) has made the PCA applicable to the U.S. Department of the Navy and the Marine Corps as a matter of DoD policy.[41] The PCA does not apply to the Coast Guard, nor does it apply to the National Guard while under Title 32 U.S.C. (state control).[42] The PCA does not contain explicit restrictions on the use of federalized militia, but the PCA does apply to the National Guard when federalized by the President under Title 10 U.S.C. (federal control).[43] Although the courts have ruled that the PCA does not apply extraterritorially and military authorities can directly enforce U.S. law outside of the United States, the DoD, as a matter of policy, applies the PCA extraterritorially.[44]

Exceptions and Additions to the Posse Comitatus Act

While the PCA was overly broad at inception it has increasingly become both ambiguous and complex due to the exception in the PCA as "expressly authorized by the Constitution or by act of Congress."[45] Congress has provided both exceptions and additional restrictions related to the PCA. The major exceptions to the PCA are found under Presidential authority granted under the Constitution and the Insurrection Statutes found in Title 10 U.S.C. Sections 331-335.[46] Additional significant exceptions are found in Title 10 U.S.C. Sections 371-382 which cover Military Support to Civilian Law Enforcement Agencies. An intrinsic exception to the PCA is the military purpose doctrine, which "allows the military to enforce civilian laws on military installations, to police themselves, and to perform their military functions even if there is an incidental benefit to civilian law enforcement."[47]

Three articles of the Constitution play a pivotal role in the use of the military for law enforcement. Article I, Section 2, of the Constitution establishes that "the President shall be the Commander in Chief of the Army and Navy of the United States, and of the Militia of the several States, when called into actual service of the United States."[48] Article II, Section 3, of the Constitution directs that the President "shall take Care that the Laws be faithfully executed."[49] And Article IV, Section 4, of the Constitution most importantly proclaims:

> The United States shall guarantee to every State in this Union a Republican Form of Government, and shall protect each of them against Invasion; and on Application of the Legislature, or of the Executive (when the Legislature cannot be convened), against domestic Violence.[50]

These three articles of the Constitution provide the President with broad responsibilities and inherent powers. While a requirement for an exception to the PCA is as "expressly authorized by the Constitution," the Supreme Court has ruled the President is not dependent on express Constitutional authorization for the exercise of powers.[51] The word "expressly" was removed from the Senate legislative PCA bill, but restored in the final bill in compromise with the House of Representatives.[52] Republican Senator Sargent provided an explanation in congressional debate on the use of the word "expressly" in the PCA:

> so that if the power arises under either the constitution or the laws it may be exercised and the Executive would not be embarrassed by the prohibition of Congress so to act where the Constitution requires him to act...but still might raise a question which he would desire to avoid if possible.[53]

While it may appear that the broad responsibilities and inherent Constitutional powers of the President always allow for the direct use of the military for law enforcement as an exception to the PCA, this is not necessarily the case, as the courts have ruled that Article IV, Section 4, of the Constitution is only provisionally effective until such time as Congress acts.[54] The President does have two direct constitutional exceptions to the PCA, identified in Title 32, Section 215.4 of the Code of Federal Regulations: emergency authority and protection of Federal property and functions.[55]

Congress did act in 1792 to provide guidance for the President to deal with domestic violence and the use of Military Assistance for Civil Disturbances through the Insurrection Act, currently codified as Title 10 U.S.C., Chapter 15, comprised of Sections 331-335.[56] Title 10 U.S.C., Sections 331-335, implement Article I, Section 8, of the Constitution, "to provide for calling forth the Militia to execute the Laws of the Union, suppress Insurrections and repel Invasions".[57] Section 331 implements Article IV, Section 4, of the Constitution, allowing the President to suppress insurrection against a state, upon request of the state, using the military.[58] Section 332 implements Article II, Section 3, of the Constitution, allowing the President to suppress rebellion against the authority of the United States.[59] Section 333 implements Article II, Section 3, and the 14th Amendment of the Constitution, allowing the President to suppress any action that interferes with state and federal law, or deprives rights of citizens--especially when a state is unable, fails, or refuses to react.[60] Section 334 requires the President to issue a proclamation to disperse, prior to the use of the military under the Insurrection Act.[61] And finally, Section 335 includes Guam and Virgin Islands as a "State" for the purposes of Title 10 U.S.C., Chapter 15.[62] These five sections that comprise the Insurrection Act provide the President direct use of the military for law enforcement as a statutory exception to the PCA.[63] The most recent use of the Insurrection Act was in April of 1992 in response to the civil unrest following the Rodney King trial in Los Angeles.[64]

Congress clarified conduct related to the PCA in providing Military Support to Civilian Law Enforcement Agencies through the 1981 Military and Civilian Law Enforcement Statute and the 1982 Defense Authorization Act, which led to the addition of Chapter 18 to Title 10 U.S.C., comprising Sections 371-382. The requirement for this act arose out of the increasing drug problem in the U.S. and the desire of Congress to increase Military Assistance to Civil Authorities.[65] Chapter 18 of Title 10 provides for increased involvement with civilian law enforcement officials in sharing information and providing support to fight the drug problem, as long as that support did not adversely affect military preparedness.[66] That support allows the military to provide directly to civilian law enforcement officials, equipment, training, access to military facilities, and support for emergency situations involving chemical or biological weapons of mass destruction.[67] Section 375 of Title 10 U.S.C. directs "that any activity under this chapter does not include or permit direct participation by a member of the Army, Navy, Air Force, or Marine Corps in a search, seizure, arrest, or other similar activity."[68] The important distinction is that this restriction only applies to those actions taken under Sections 371-382 of Title 10 U.S.C. and does not apply otherwise. Section 379 of Title 10 U.S.C. provides a method for the Navy to avoid violating the PCA while conducting drug-interdiction missions by placing law enforcement qualified Coast Guard members on Navy ships.[69] Under Title 10 U.S.C., Section 382 the military can render assistance to civilian law enforcement agencies on chemical and biological weapons, and under Title 18 U.S.C., Section 831 the military can assist the Department of Justice concerning nuclear weapons.[70]

The Nunn-Lugar-Domenici Amendment and National Defense Authorization Act of 1997 directed the DoD to create a training program and develop a military based domestic terrorism rapid response team with a capability for detection, neutralization, containment, dismantlement, and disposal of WMD.[71] The USA PATRIOT ACT of 2001 and the Homeland Security Act of 2002 increased the role of the military in homeland security.[72] Section 886 of the Homeland Security Act of 2002 entitled "Sense of Congress Reaffirming the Continued Importance and Applicability of the Posse Comitatus Act," confirmed the basis and continued importance of the PCA.[73]

Indirect involvement of the military in law enforcement activities is permitted as long as the military has "not subjected civilians to the exercise of military power that is regulatory, proscriptive, or compulsory in nature."[74] This allows the military to provide equipment, transportation, training, supplies, and services to law enforcement officials as long as it does "not directly and actively participate in law enforcement tasks."[75] Providing advice by the military to law enforcement officials is also permitted as long as the military does "not actively pervade the activities of the civilian authorities."[76] The tests of not subjecting civilians to the exercise of military power that is regulatory, proscriptive, or compulsory in nature; not directly and actively participating in law enforcement tasks; and not actively pervading the activities of the civilian authorities represent the three tests used by the courts to determine whether violations of the PCA have occurred.[77] These tests arose out of federal court cases over the involvement of the military in the FBI siege at Wounded Knee from February to May of 1973.[78]

Congress also enacted specific exceptions to the PCA allowing the military to provide disaster relief and protection of public health and safety under the Robert T. Stafford Disaster Relief Act enacted in Title 42 U.S.C. Section 5170b.[79] The Stafford Act gives the President broad discretion to find that a major disaster exists, requiring emergency response after a declaration request from the Governor of the affected state.[80] Once the President has declared an emergency or major disaster and invoked the Stafford Act, the Governor of the affected state can request use of the resources of the DoD for emergency work that is essential for the preservation of life and property.[81] The DoD can provide military support to include clearance and removal of debris and wreckage, and temporary restoration of essential public facilities and services for up to 10 days under the Stafford Act.[82]

7

Title 32, Section 215.4 of the Code of Federal Regulations only identifies six exceptions to the PCA, two constitutional and four statutory, of which all but one statutory exception for support of the Secret Service are discussed above.[83] In a 2000 report, the Congressional Research Service identified 24 total statutory exceptions to the PCA.[84] The 2001 USA PATRIOT ACT effectively added another statutory exception by increasing the ability of the military to support civil authorities in responding to WMD.[85] One final additional exception worthy of discussion is found in the concept of martial law.

Ignorance and careless diction, even more so than for the PCA, applies to martial law.[86] Between the movies and the media, martial law is bantered about to create an impression of substance.[87] Martial law is more about what does not exist, than what does--it is the absence of order, courts, and constitution that define the environment of martial law.[88] Martial law is the use of force by the military to maintain order by acting as the police, the court, and the legislature.[89] The Supreme Court Case, *ex parte Milligan*, provided guidance on martial law and arose out of a case that occurred during the Civil War involving a Confederate sympathizer sentenced to death by a military commission.[90] The Court ruled, "Martial law ... destroys every guarantee of the Constitution," specifically in this case with no habeas corpus. The Court also ruled, "Civil liberty and this kind of martial law cannot endure together; the antagonism is irreconcilable; and, in the conflict, one or the other must perish."[91] Title 32, Section 501.4, of the Code of Federal Regulations, as the only statutory reference on martial law, implements the rulings of the Court in *ex parte Milligan* and establishes that the President predominantly declares martial law and that it is driven by necessity.[92] It is unlikely that deploying the military under the Insurrection Act will require invoking martial law as the proper role of the military in this case is to support, not supplant, civil authority.[93] The litmus test of the Court for martial law is the functioning of the courts themselves.[94] If the courts are open then martial law is not appropriate. Martial law is most appropriate during war concerning captured territory without a functioning government. After the fall of the Iraqi government during Operation IRAQI FREEDOM, martial law was declared and the U.S. military assumed the responsibilities of the central government.

Adding to the confusion that Congress created by statutory exceptions and additions related to the PCA, the DoD has created an even more confusing collection of directives related to the PCA that strongly reinforces the PCA. The construct of the DoD collection of directives related to the PCA, comprising Department of Defense Directive (DoDD) 3025.1, Military Support to Civil Authorities, 1993; DoDD 3025.12, Military Assistance for Civil Disturbances, 1994; DoDD 3025.15, Military Assistance to Civil Authorities, 1997; and DoDD 5525.5, DoD

Cooperation with Civilian Law Enforcement Officials, 1986; does not correctly align with Joint Doctrine established by Joint Publication 3-26, Homeland Security by titles, let alone content.[95] The DoD directives are not up to date, with the oldest directive over 20 years old, and quoting an obsolete version of the PCA from 1959. The directives somewhat recreate a standalone "PCA" in themselves by specifying content and/or intent of many of the related PCA constitutional and statutory exceptions and restrictions, rather than consistently providing references to the applicable Constitution Article, United States Code, or Code of Federal Regulations.[96] The DoD policy related to the PCA also appears to advance another exception to the PCA.

DoDD 5525.5 created some of the previously discussed exceptions to the PCA, not by law, but by policy. This directive extends the PCA extraterritorially, now requiring compelling and extraordinary circumstances to submit a request to the Secretary of Defense for an exception to this policy. This directive also extends the PCA to apply to the Department of the Navy and the Marine Corps. Additionally DoDD 5525.5 exceeds the congressional intent of Title 10, Section 375 providing restrictions beyond those specified therein.

The four separate DoD Directives together identify another exception of "Immediate Response Authority" in two of the directives and a similar "emergency authority" in the other two directives. The immediate response authority is also identified in JP 3-26 and anticipated in the next version of JP 1-02. These two similar policies are essentially the implementation of Title 32 C.F.R. Section 215.4 and the parallel Title 32 C.F.R. Sections 501.2 and 501.5.

There is a suggestion that the DoD is reticent, through policy, to participate in providing Military Support to Law Enforcement Agencies by the language used in DoDD 5525.5 and respective service directives (SECNAVINST 5820.7B, AFI 10-801, and AR 500-51) with the phrases "extent practical" and "maximum extent practicable," respectively, when discussing the criteria used to provide support.[97] JP 3-26, observes that "Since [Civil Support] is not DoD's primary mission, all requests for DoD military assistance are evaluated against the following criteria: legality, readiness, lethality, risk, cost, and appropriateness."[98] JP 3-26 also specifies that the "DoD shall cooperate with and provide support to civil authorities as directed by and consistent with laws, Presidential directives, [Executive Orders], and DoD policies and directives." Congress has clearly indicated their intentions through Title 10 U.S.C. Sections 371-382 that Military Support to Civilian Law Enforcement Agencies will occur.

The Congressional and DoD exceptions and additions related to the PCA establish the PCA as the central issue in the U.S. military providing Military Assistance to Civil Authorities. The image of the PCA as representing the hub of a wagon wheel is easily imagined (see

9

figure 1). The spokes of the wagon wheel and the rim of the wheel all support the hub and its ultimate purpose of supporting the wagon, which in this case represents the Constitution and the requirement "to ensure domestic tranquility, provide for the common defense, promote the general Welfare, and secure the Blessings of Liberty to ourselves and our Posterity."[99] The individual spokes of the wagon wheel represent the range of varied exceptions, additions, and policy reinforcements to the PCA making for very many irregular spokes. The rim or outer surface of the wagon wheel, with the PCA as the central issue, logically represents in this model the requirement of the U.S. military to provide support to civil authorities. The rim ensures the integrity of the entire wagon and allows it to function as a wagon. The irregular spokes of the wheel form an irregular shaped rim, making it rather rough for the requirement of the U.S. military to provide support to civil authorities. This irregular shaped rim is the object of friction and takes the potential for wear, compromise, and in some cases material failure. The road surface condition represents the challenges to the operation of the wagon with a smooth paved surface under clear, dry conditions equating to peace, and a potholed, rough surface on a dark and stormy night equating to a crisis caused by natural disaster, terrorist attack, or civil unrest.

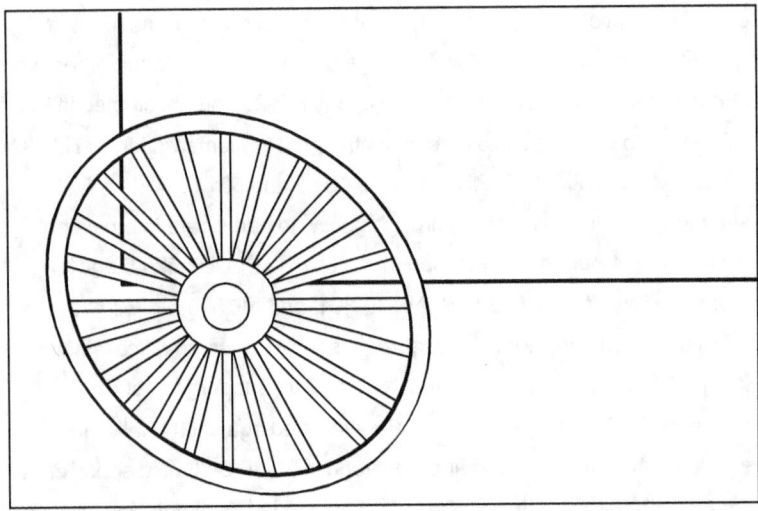

FIGURE 1. WAGON MODEL OF THE PCA.

Hurricane Katrina and the PCA

On Sunday, August 28, 2005, Hurricane Katrina, a very large category 5 storm, directly approached New Orleans, Louisiana. Even prior to landfall, President Bush had signed the emergency declaration and the Stafford Act was in effect, and FEMA, now an agency within the Department of Homeland Security, was pre-positioning materials to immediately respond after the storm passed.[100] As Hurricane Katrina made landfall on Monday, August 29, 2005, slightly to the East of New Orleans, the storm was downgraded to a category 3 hurricane. In spite of the seemingly beneficial shift in direction and intensity, Hurricane Katrina resulted in catastrophic destruction of the Gulf Coast of Mississippi and the greater New Orleans area. The Mississippi Gulf Coast suffered the direct brunt of the 27 foot storm surge and category 3 winds. Even though New Orleans escaped a direct hit, the levee system in New Orleans unfortunately failed in three locations putting 80% of the city under six to twenty feet of water. The response across the board to the aftermath of Hurricane Katrina is more about what did not happen than what did happen.

The New Orleans City government was immediately rendered ineffective in operations and communications, unable to provide a reliable assessment and response to the aftermath of Hurricane Katrina. The Mayor of New Orleans, Ray Nagin, operated out of the New Orleans Hyatt Hotel after Hurricane Katrina's landfall and was unable to establish reliable communications for nearly forty-eight hours. The Mayor was unable to effectively command the local efforts and guide the State and Federal support for two days following the storm.[101]

The Governor of Louisiana, Kathleen Babineaux Blanco, contacted the White House on Monday evening and spoke to President Bush asking, "Mr. President, we need your help. We need everything you've got."[102] What followed was the largest response ever to a natural disaster. Initially 4,000 Louisiana National Guard troops deployed prior to landfall, and in immediate response to the aftermath a total of 5,804 were serving by Tuesday, August 30, 2005. Due to the size of the response required, NORTHCOM established a joint task force, JTF-Katrina, with Lieutenant General Russel Honore, the Defense Coordinating Officer, as the Task Force Commander.

By the time President Bush arrived in New Orleans on Friday, September 2, 2005 to meet with Governor Blanco and Mayor Nagin aboard Air Force One, in Louisiana alone there were 12,224 National Guard troops serving with 5,445 of those coming from other states through the Emergency Management Assistance Compact (EMAC).[103] Aboard Air Force One a heated discussion occurred, that was described "as blunt as you can get without the Secret Service getting involved," between President Bush, Governor Blanco, and Mayor Nagin, about the failures of the federal response and over the question of who was in charge.[104] At one point Nagin slammed his hand down on the table and told Bush, "We just need to cut through this and do what it takes to have a more-controlled command structure. If that means federalizing it, let's do it."[105] Nagin suggested Lt. Gen. Honore take charge and the President asked Gov. Blanco her opinion, to which she asked for a private conversation. One can only deduce the contents

11

of that private conversation from the reported communication that evening from the White House to the Governor asking her to request a federal takeover and possible use of the Insurrection Act.[106] Her request never came. The President demonstrated a policy of not preempting state control in even the most dire of circumstances. While politics did play into the equation, given a Republican President and Democratic Governor, the Constitution was prominently a player if not by choice, then by chance.

An alternative command structure for the military response to the aftermath of Hurricane Katrina was proposed by the White House, but rejected by the Louisiana Governor's office.[107] The President and the governor of an affected state can both authorize a state National Guard commander under Title 10 status to retain Title 32 authority. In this dual-hat capacity, the National Guard commander reports to both the governor (for state requirements) and the supported combatant commander (for DoD mission assignments), and can have Title 10 forces placed under their command, through an interplay of Title 32 U.S.C. Section 315 and Title 32 U.S.C Section 325.[108] This would have provided the essence of unity of command for JTF-Katrina, but still with the potential for conflict between the Governor and NORTHCOM Commander.

By September 7, 2005, 42,990 National Guard troops, 17,417 Active Duty troops, 20 U.S. ships, 360 helicopters, and 93 fixed wing aircraft had responded to the affected area.[109] The military chain of command during the response to the aftermath of Hurricane Katrina remained separate for the National Guard and Active Duty, with the National Guard reporting to the Governor through The Adjutant General (TAG) for the respective state, and the Active Duty reporting to the JTF-Katrina Commander, Lt. Gen. Russell Honore.[110] With the exception of the evacuations of the Superdome and the Convention Center in New Orleans, the separate commands divided the area of operations geographically and supported response efforts separately.[111] This arrangement did allow for the National Guard, who was providing the majority of military forces responding to the aftermath of Hurricane Katrina, to provide law enforcement as the PCA did not apply. Unity of command was not obtained, but unity of effort was evident.[112] Unfortunately a catastrophic major disaster demands unity of command, while an emergency requires unity of effort.

Some situations encountered during the overwhelming aftermath of Hurricane Katrina prevented the National Guard from executing the law enforcement mission even with the legal authorization to do so. When the New Orleans Convention Center turned into an impromptu unplanned and unorganized refugee center, 222 Corps of Engineer soldiers locked themselves into a separate exhibit hall rather than face the angry and desperate crowd of more than

10,000.[113] Colonel Douglas Mouton, Commander of the Louisiana National Guard's 225th Engineering Group, personally made the painful decision not to respond given the situation of "a partially armed group of engineers, ready to operate equipment, and with enough food and water to anger 20,000 people."[114] Without the training and resources required to respond to a specific situation, statutory guidance was useless and on the spot policy making saved the day from making an ugly situation a possible constitutional crisis.

Ignorance and careless diction were rampant during the response to Hurricane Katrina, none more so than concerning martial law at the local level and within the press. Even after the Louisiana State Attorney General on Tuesday, August 30, 2005, clarified press reports that martial law was declared in parts of southeast Louisiana, saying no such term exists in Louisiana law, local officials continued to claim and the press continued to report that martial law was in effect.[115] Mayor Nagin claimed and the press reported on Wednesday, August 31, 2005, that martial law was in effect.[116] On Wednesday, September 7, 2005, the city's superintendent of police, P. Edwin Compass III, claimed and the New York Times reported, "There's a martial law declaration in place that gives us legal authority for mandatory evacuations."[117] One press story on September 2, 2005 incorrectly claimed that the PCA limited the President's power to declare martial law.[118] Even the highest levels of government were not exempt from ignorance and careless diction, for on Wednesday, September 2, 2005, Scott McClellan, the White House press secretary, told a group of reporters that, "martial law has been declared in Mississippi and Louisiana."[119] After Hurricane Katrina there was absolutely no cause for consideration of martial law at the federal level since the local courts were open and available.[120]

The overall lessons learned from the aftermath of Hurricane Katrina were captured in the February 2006 White House report on the federal response to Hurricane Katrina. The report reiterated the President's request in September 2005 for Congress to consider "greater federal authority and a broader role for the armed forces" in responding to a natural disaster:[121]

> The Departments of Homeland Security and Defense should jointly plan for the Department of Defense's support of Federal response activities as well as those extraordinary circumstances when it is appropriate for the Department of Defense to lead the Federal response. In addition, the Department of Defense should ensure the transformation of the National Guard is focused on increased integration with active duty forces for homeland security plans and activities.[122]

The President's policy clearly sees the military playing the leading role in responding to catastrophic natural disasters and terrorist attacks. This brings the PCA back into question on the role it will play in allowing the President to implement that policy.

13

Options for the Posse Comitatus Act

The applicability of the PCA in light of the history of constitutional and statutory exceptions combined with recent and potential domestic events demands a review of options for the PCA and all related exceptions, additions, and reinforcements with a discussion of the merits of those options. The three basic options are to repeal the PCA, leave the PCA "as-is", or to modify the PCA.

Repealing the Posse Comitatus Act

Repeal of the PCA outright has merits in that it provides flexibility to use the military in a law enforcement role to support national security. [123] No one has ever been convicted of violating the PCA indicating its uselessness as a criminal statute and supporting repeal.[124] There is clearly a disconnect between the domestic environment of the late eighteenth century when the PCA was written and today. [125] Deputy Secretary Paul Wolfowitz, testifying before the Senate Armed Services Committee shortly after the events of September 11, 2001, strongly favored a review of the PCA in agreement with Senator John Warner. [126] Wolfowitz indicated that the attacks on the World Trade Center and the Pentagon have allowed for Americans to envision terrorist attacks in which the military would have unique response capabilities, particularly in response to a chemical or biological weapon.[127] Senator Carl Levin in October 2001, as Chairman of the U.S. Senate Committee on Armed Services, brought up the question of repealing or revising the PCA in discussing the role of the Department of Defense in homeland security. [128]

The PCA does remain a significant obstacle to unified action on homeland security. [129] The PCA combined with constitutional and statutory exceptions have created a complicated environment for military and political leaders to respond to real world events that demands advice of counsel before taking action.[130] The PCA has too many interpretations of its application and the predictably conservative advice of counsel does not lend itself to effective and timely military action.[131] The legislative patchwork is haphazard at best and an effective strategy requires at least unity of effort and more optimally unity of command.[132] Focusing narrowly on the law enforcement aspect fails the legitimate expectation of homeland security. [133] The Los Angeles riots in April 1992, following the acquittal of police officers accused of beating Rodney King, provoked a Presidential order authorizing federal troops to stop the domestic violence.[134] The Joint Task Force commander refused law enforcement missions due to belief that the PCA was a constraint when it was not since the Constitutional and Insurrection Act exceptions to the PCA applied.[135] The President ordered lawful action the Joint Task Force commander failed to carry out. In this case the end result was still acceptable as just the presence of the military had a stabilizing effect, but future crises may not have the same outcome with a misapplication of the PCA.

Homeland security previously had little attention or priority in national security policy. [136] The global economy, the revolution in information technology, and other technology advances have added a new dimension to the homeland security paradigm.[137] Previously homeland security was a defensive and reactive issue; now it requires an offensive and proactive focus.[138] Terrorism is a clear and present danger today and we do not have the luxury of unlimited time in erecting the necessary defenses with restrictive legislation blocking the way. [139] The current operating environment may not allow ample time for an act of Congress or Presidential declaration of emergency to provide safety and protection, nor to prevent and deter acts of terror using the military. [140] The PCA stands as somewhat of an impediment to agility and adaptability of the military to national defense given the byzantine nature of the PCA with all of the exceptions and additions.[141]

Law enforcement is incapable of exclusively managing the threat nor solely capable of responding to the consequences of catastrophic acts within the U.S. homeland.[142] The military has inherent capability and organization structure to respond to national security interests and the organic assets of the DoD can provide immediate internal defense in response to terrorism or natural disasters.[143] The military maintains many of the tools and the skills needed to deal with the threat to homeland security. [144] Repeal of the PCA would allow for direct application of those tools and skills. The PCA makes it very difficult for continuous combined arms, joint, interagency, coalition and multi-dimensional operations which are prerequisites for success in the war on terror or responding to natural disasters.[145]

The response of the military to Hurricane Katrina is an indication that the military has a stand-alone capability beyond any other organization to respond to a catastrophic terrorist or natural disaster event. The Department of Defense response to Hurricane Katrina was the largest, fastest deployment of military forces for a civil-support mission in U.S. history and unprecedented in size and scope not only in the U.S., but also in the world.[146] The military provides for better defense of the homeland, but troops alone will not accomplish the desired effect as other security measures must accompany it to include: interagency coordination, command and control, and unity of command. The strategic context demonstrates the need to overcome the PCA to preserve national values and national purpose.[147] With the obvious increase in missions that would come with repeal of the PCA must come corresponding training and funding to help mitigate negative aspects.

While all the arguments above make a strong case for repealing the PCA, there are very serious constitutional issues with repealing the PCA, as it could appear as a power grab by the President, and establish a sense of what was previously an emergency power as now status quo.[148] The conservative The Washington Times characterized the PCA in an editorial as "a barrier against the pell-mell deployment of troops by the President against the American people."[149] The PCA fundamentally protects the nation from the danger of a military dictatorship.[150] While a military coup in the U.S. is highly unlikely, it is still necessary to preserve the historic division between military and civilian roles.[151] Repealing the PCA could undermine civilian control of the military, making it difficult to maintain a subordinate role over the long-term.[152] The New York Times identified the PCA as "an important bulwark of civilian supremacy and a barrier to the erosion of basic civil liberties."[153]

The direct involvement of the military in law enforcement has serious potential for infringement on individual rights.[154] The military does not currently have a skill set optimal for law enforcement and is not necessarily trained to uphold the rights to privacy and due process.[155] The character of law enforcement de-escalates to use lesser forms of force while the military escalates to use deadly force in accomplishing the mission.[156] Simply put, law enforcement personnel search and capture, while the military search and destroy. [157] An incident in 1997 demonstrates the tragic consequences that can occur when the military directly interacts with the civilian population during mission execution: a Marine surveillance team conducting a counter-drug mission near the Texas-Mexico border shot and killed an 18-year-old boy tending the family goat herd when they felt threatened.[158] Incidents of this type fuel the remnants of the colonial fear of direct military involvement in domestic affairs.[159] The issues surrounding the Abu Ghraib prisoner abuse incidents do not help the argument for repeal of the PCA either.

Opening the military to domestic law enforcement could dilute the primary mission which is already facing a demanding operations tempo.[160] The domestic law enforcement mission would take resources and training time away from preparing for the primary mission. [161] Over reliance on the military for homeland security may reduce the military's primary mission capability to support U.S. foreign policy. [162] In addition, it could soften the warrior mentality and ultimately reduce the respect of citizens for the military which would reverse a long standing trend.[163]

Looking at the wagon model and the effect of repealing the PCA, equates to removing the hub which compromises the wagon wheel, and the wagon does not function (see Figure 2). Repealing the PCA also requires the deconstruction of all the statutory exceptions and restrictions. This equates to disassembly of the spokes of the wheel and putting the remaining axle on a jack stand. The military now represents the jack stand and the direct support of the wagon, which is not especially functional.

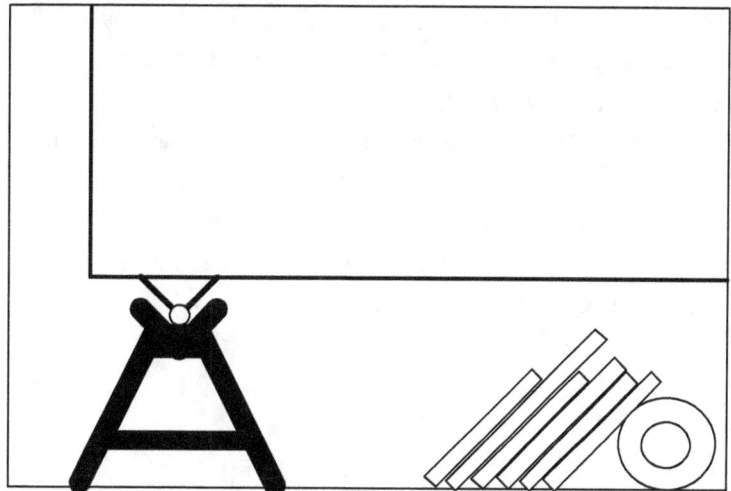

FIGURE 2. WAGON MODEL WITH REPEAL OF THE PCA

Leaving the Posse Comitatus Act "as-is"

Leaving the PCA "as-is" has inherent limits. The PCA is now just a procedural formality rather than an actual impediment due to the gradual erosion of the basic restriction due to the many statutory exceptions.[164] Even though Congress provided legislation that eroded the PCA, and the exceptions granted to the PCA provide the ability to use the military in most conceivable emergency situations, the PCA and related statutory exceptions still restricts the military from direct law enforcement which the homeland security mission may require.[165]

A perfect example of this restriction occurred during the military response to Hurricane Andrew. The troops did not take action when faced with law enforcement issues as they were Active Duty forces under Title 10 U.S. Code and were complying with the PCA.[166] Even during periods of localized lawlessness in an apparently failed city within the conterminous United States the military in this case was legally powerless to take action. The majority of the troops responding to Hurricane Katrina did not come under the PCA, but a significant portion of the military forces responding were still under the restrictions of the PCA.

Leaving the PCA "as-is" is maintaining the status quo. While the many exceptions have weakened the PCA, it still remains a deterrent to using the military in response to what is purely a civilian law enforcement matter.[167] Leaving the PCA "as-is" may require additional legislation to circumvent the PCA, as it may not fully satisfy security requirements given emerging threats to national security demanding changes.[168]  Under the absolute worst of circumstances, we may see Déjà vu all over again requiring Presidential suspension of law.[169]  When President Lincoln suspended the writ of habeas corpus in 1861 for the public safety, in a special message to Congress on July 4, 1861, he asked, "all the laws, but one, to go unexecuted, and the government itself to go to pieces, lest that one be violated?"[170]

In the wagon model, leaving the PCA and related exceptions "as-is" maintains the status quo and has the wagon marginally functional relative to extreme dynamic conditions (see Figure 3).  Even under the best of road surface conditions the wagon wheel function is questionable.  The wagon works as history shows, but unanticipated conditions may challenge the functionality of the wagon through stress on the wheel and hub.

FIGURE 3.  WAGON MODEL LEAVING THE PCA "AS-IS"

Modifying the Posse Comitatus Act

Modifying the PCA is dependent on changes that would bring clarity and appropriateness to the act.  At a minimum the PCA should change from a criminal statute in Title 32 U.S.C. to an organic statute in Title 10 U.S.C. as the erosion over the years, combined with no convictions, has circumvented its usefulness.[171]  The lack of successful prosecutions under the PCA causes the law to lack force and credibility.[172]  Recodification into Title 10 U.S.C. brings the PCA into line with its current function and force as a law of policy, in both application and political discourse as a limitation on the use of the military, rather than a law of crime.[173]  Retaining the PCA as legislation, albeit modified, maintains flexibility, yet there are still constraints on the use

18

of the military by Congress and the President.[174]  Mathew Hammond in the Washington University Law Quarterly proposed the following Title 10 U.S.C. recodification of the PCA:

> (a) Any part of the armed forces, excluding the Coast Guard, is prohibited from acting as a *posse comitatus* or otherwise to execute the laws, except in cases and under circumstances expressly authorized by the Constitution or Act of Congress.
>
> (b) Exceptions to paragraph (a) allowing use of the armed forces must meet the following criteria:
>
>> (1) the use must be triggered by an emergency, which is defined as any occasion or instance for which Federal assistance is needed to supplement State and local efforts and capabilities to save lives and to protect property and public health and safety, or to lessen or avert the threat of a catastrophe--generally a sudden, unexpected event;
>>
>> (2) the use must be beyond the capabilities of civilian authorities; and
>>
>> (3) the use must be one limited in duration and not one which addresses a chronic, continuing issue or problem.
>
> (c) Clarifications to prohibitions in subsection (a) are to be made by regulations to be published in the Federal Register and printed in the Code of Federal Regulations.
>
> (d) This section is an affirmation of the fundamental precept of the United States of separating the military and civilian spheres of authority.
>
> (e) Nothing in this section shall be construed to affect the law enforcement functions of the United States Coast Guard.[175]

The language in subsection (a) above is similar to the current wording in the PCA and establishes a continuation of the PCA leaving some of the ambiguity and vagueness.  Problems occur in addressing chronic issues, such as counterdrug, border security, and terrorism which all come under the homeland security mission and the purview of the Department of Homeland Security.

A base line above the status quo is established by the modified PCA removing previous exceptions or making them all the more difficult to accomplish, but the modified PCA clarifies the law and lessens the need for exceptions while providing military commanders with guidance.[176]  With world events stretching military resources and with increasing demands on military budgets, a decrease in Military Assistance to Civil Authority missions could provide some budget relief.  Counterdrug and border security issues do not pose an acute catastrophic potential while the terrorism threat does, and the modified PCA could pass the test there based upon subsection (b) in planning and responding to acute terrorist attacks.  Modifying the PCA would compel the Department of Homeland Security to develop more robust and completely organic capabilities to meet the requirements of the counterdrug and border security missions.

The complete list of statutory exceptions would require review to ensure compliance with the modified PCA. For example, modifying the PCA would require revision to Title 10 U.S.C. Sections 371-382 that would strictly limit Military Support to Law Enforcement Agencies. Complete revision to the DoD and service directives related to the PCA is also necessitated by modifying the PCA, but they are due for review and revision regardless.

Modifying the PCA provides the potential for all of the armed forces to participate in law enforcement. An event would have to exceed the threshold that demands a declaration of emergency before the military could participate in a law enforcement role under the modified PCA. Both active and reserve components of all the military departments could execute the law enforcement mission once an emergency is declared. Modifying the PCA improves the responsiveness of the military to the law enforcement mission once an emergency is declared.

However, the valid argument for retaining the essential elements of the PCA and related exceptions, which currently allow for ongoing military involvement in counterdrug and border security missions, centers around the potential for homeland security failure. Under the modified PCA, a major component of that potential for homeland security failure is the inability to use National Guard troops for law enforcement purposes for non-emergency events, both at the state and federal level, outside of invoking a statutory exception such as the Insurrection Act. The downside is that not employing the most powerful military in the world, in a domestic role to assure national security, could have tragic consequences.[177]

Modifying the PCA and related exceptions is symbolized in the wagon model as providing a uniform and round wagon wheel with fewer, stronger spokes and a more robust hub (see Figure 4). The uniformity of the wagon wheel allows for the wagon to better tolerate varied conditions of the road. This viewpoint makes it readily apparent in the wagon model that the hub, the PCA, is not the problem; the too numerous irregular spokes are the problem. Instead of many irregular spokes, the wagon wheel should consist of fewer uniform spokes that will increase the functionality of the rim. Instead of an irregular shaped rim that only works marginally well in the best of conditions--on a dry, straight improved road of very uniform surface at a slow speed--we obtain a uniformly round rim that can tolerate and adapt to the worst of conditions, on a slippery, curved, unimproved road with potholes, at any speed.

20

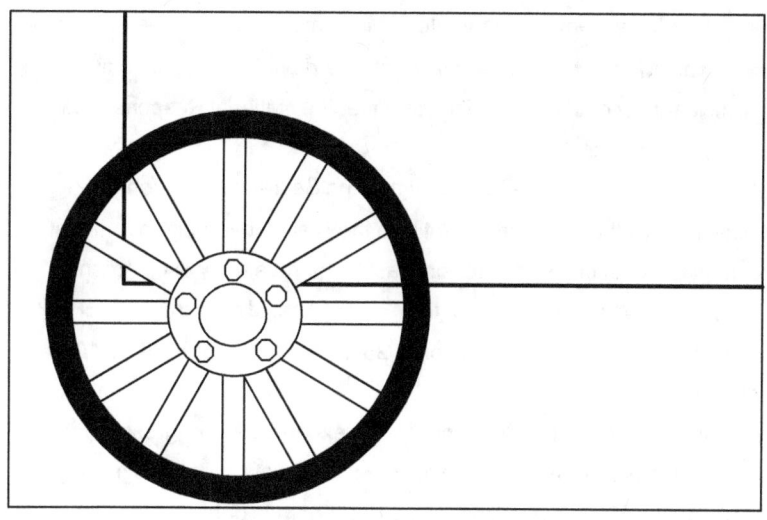

FIGURE 4.  WAGON MODEL WITH MODIFIED PCA

Conclusion

The Military Assistance to Civil Authorities mission is driven more by policy than statutory guidance as evidenced by the inherent constitutional powers of the President in spite of the PCA.  The events after Hurricane Katrina demonstrate the application of policy by the President as necessary to respond to the realities of a major disaster at operational and political levels.  The directives implementing the DoD policy on Military Assistance to Civil Authorities adds another component of power over and above statutory guidance.

At a minimum the DoD policy should change to match Congressional intent with appropriate revision to PCA related DoD and service directives, specifically those involving Military Assistance to Civil Authorities.  The Office of the Secretary of Defense (OSD) should consider consolidating the four PCA related directives into one single directive with subsections aligned with the CS mission subsets as defined in JP 3-26, and also provide clarity on constitutional and statutory guidance by reference rather than by paraphrase or quote.  The OSD should also direct the respective services to rewrite the corresponding instructions and regulations to achieve the same.[178]

Congress should give serious consideration to modifying the PCA to recodify the act from a criminal statute in Title 18 to an organic statute in Title 10, and to clarify the limitations to apply to chronic issues.  This will require an expansion of capability for the Department of Homeland Security to deal with chronic issues related to border security and counterdrug operations.  The modified PCA though, will not prevent the President from dealing with acute issues and

21

employing the military in a broader law enforcement role. With a modified PCA, the President should consider a policy of placing under Title 10 all National Guard personnel responding to emergencies designated incidents of national significance under the National Response Plan in order to provide a pure unity of command.

In the absence of modifying the PCA, the President and the Secretary of Defense (SECDEF) should consider a policy that has agreement with the State Governors to dual-hat the respective State TAG during a natural disaster or terrorist act to improve unity of command. During acute situations requiring invoking the Insurrection Act, the President and SECDEF should consider a policy of placing all responding National Guard personnel under Title 10 to attain a pure unity of command.

In the case of any changes made to the PCA and related exceptions, Congress must apply due care to balance the requirements of reality with the concept of civilian and military separation. Supreme Court Justice Robert Jackson once said, "There is danger that, if the court does not temper its doctrinaire logic with a little practical wisdom, it will convert the constitutional Bill of Rights into a suicide pact."[179] That concept matches Secretary of Defense Donald H. Rumsfeld's observation on the PCA that "common sense and national need sometimes make military assistance necessary."[180] Justice Jackson also cautioned though not "to emphasize transient results upon policies and lose sight of enduring consequences upon the balanced structure of our Republic."[181] Major George S. Patton, Jr., Cavalry, tenaciously understood the issue concerning Military Assistance to Civil Authorities when he wrote in 1932:

> We, of the Army, should take pride in the fact that not once in all of these cases have our predecessors either failed or been guilty of unnecessary violence. It must be our aim to maintain this proud tradition whenever it shall be our unfortunate duty to be called on for such onerous service.

> Remember that when the Army has done its duty, liberty has flourished and that when it has failed, riot has changed into rebellion. Indeed, the epitaphs of those countless nations dead of the suicide of insurrection should bear these words, "DIED THIS DATE DUE TO THE FAILURE OF IT'S SOLDIERS."

The caveat Senator Gary Hart correctly pointed out is that in the case of a "catastrophic attack of some kind, obviously, every asset in this country is going to come into play. Nobody's going to be worrying about the niceties of the Posse Comitatus Act."[182] The Latin phrase, Inter arma silent leges, "in times of war, law is silent", emphasizes the need to take action before reaction is required. It is therefore incumbent on Congress, the President, and the DoD to create a policy environment where the U.S. military can provide rapid and decisive support to civil authorities in a crisis, like the aftermath of Hurricane Katrina, and especially in response to

22

our worst fear--catastrophic destruction of a major U.S. city following a successful terrorist attack involving WMD--yet not undermine the foundation of the country, the U.S. Constitution.

Endnotes

[1] *Use of Army and Air Force as Posse Comitatus*, U.S. Code, vol. 18, sec. 1385; available from http://frwebgate.access.gpo.gov/cgi-bin/getdoc.cgi?dbname=browse_usc&docid=Cite:+18USC1385; Internet; accessed 08 December 2005.

[2] COL Dana K. Chipman, *Countering Terrorism in the Heartland – Can We Afford Posse Comitatus Any Longer?* (Carlisle Barracks: U.S. Army War College, 04 July 2003), 12; available from http://handle.dtic.mil/100.2/ADA415647; Internet; accessed 13 March 2006.

[3] U.S. Department of Energy, *President Discusses Hurricane Effects on Energy Supply* (Washington, D.C.: U.S. Department of Energy, 26 September 2005); available from http://www.whitehouse.gov/news/releases/2005/09/20050926.html; Internet; accessed 19 February 2006.

[4] George S. Patton, Jr., "Federal Troops in Domestic Disturbances," November 1932; available from http://www.pattonhq.com/textfiles/federal.htm; Internet; accessed 03 March 2006.

[5] Charles M. Province, *The Unknown Patton* (n.p.: CMP Publications, 2002), 52; available from http://www.pattonhq.com/unknownpdf.html; Internet; accessed 13 March 2006.

[6] Alfred H. Kelly and Winfred A. Harbison, *The American Constitution: Its Origins and Development* (New York: W.W. Norton and Company, Inc, 1963), 82, 176.

[7] Ibid., 89.

[8] Ibid., 100-101.

[9] Ibid., 108.

[10] Ibid., 114-160.

[11] Ibid., 174-177.

[12] Ibid., 166.

[13] Matthew Carlton Hammond, "The Posse Comitatus Act: A Principle in Need of Renewal," *Washington University Law Quarterly* 75 (Summer 1997) [journal on-line]; available from http://law.wustl.edu/WULQ/75-2/752-10.html; Internet; accessed 10 November 2005.

[14] Stephen Young, "The Posse Comitatus Act: A Resource Guide," *Law Library Resource Xchange*, 17 February 2003 [journal on-line]; available from http://www.llrx.com/features/posse.htm; Internet; accessed 24 January 2006.

[15] Ibid.

[16] Ibid.

[17] Ibid.

[18] Ibid.

[19] Ibid; U.S. Constitution, Bill of Rights: Amendment I - Congress shall make no law respecting an establishment of religion, or prohibiting the free exercise thereof; or abridging the freedom of speech, or of the press; or the right of the people peaceably to assemble, and to petition the government for a redress of grievances.  Amendment IV - The right of the people to be secure in their persons, houses, papers, and effects, against unreasonable searches and seizures, shall not be violated, and no warrants shall issue, but upon probable cause, supported by oath or affirmation, and particularly describing the place to be searched, and the persons or things to be seized;  available from http://www.house.gov/Constitution/Amend.html; Internet; accessed 08 December 2005

[20] Ibid.

[21] \Pos"se com`i*ta"tus\ [L. posse to be able, to have power + LL. comitatus a county, from comes, comitis, a count. See County, and Power.] 1. (Law) The power of the county, or the citizens who may be summoned by the sheriff to assist the authorities in suppressing a riot, or executing any legal precept which is forcibly opposed. –Blackstone, available from http://dictionary.reference.com/search?q=posse%20comitatus; Internet; accessed 22 February 2006.

[22] Gerald J. Manley, *The Posse Comitatus Act Post-9/11: Time for a Change?* (Washington, D.C.: National Defense University, National War College, 2003), 2; available from www.ndu.edu/library/n4/n03AManleyPosse.pdf; Internet; accessed 13 March 2006.

[23] Charles Doyle, *The Posse Comitatus Act and Related Matters: The Use of the Military to Execute Civilian Law* (Washington, D.C.: Congressional Research Service, The Library of Congress, 01 June 2000), 6; available from www.fas.org/sgp/crs/natsec/95-964.pdf; Internet; accessed 13 March 2006.

[24] U.S. Department of the Army, *Stability Operations and Support Operations*, Field Manual 3-07 (Washington, D.C.: U.S. Department of the Army, February 2003), 6-7; available from https://atiam.train.army.mil/soldierPortal/atia/adlsc/view/public/9630-1/fm/3-07/fm3_07.pdf; Internet; accessed 13 March 2006.

[25] Doyle, 7-9.

[26] Ibid., 9.  See also 6 Op. Att'y Gen. 466, 473 (1854).  This opinion is known as the Cushing Doctrine which the PCA overturned.

[27] MAJ Jeffery K. Toomer, A *Strategic View of Homeland Security: Relooking the Posse Comitatus Act and DOD's Role in Homeland Security* (Fort Leavenworth: U.S. Army Command and General Staff College, 2002), 12-13; available from http://handle.dtic.mil/100.2/ADA403866; Internet; accessed 13 March 2006.

[28] Chipman, 5.

[29] COL Nolon J. Benson, Jr., *The Posse Comitatus Act: Is There a Need for Change?*, (Carlisle Barracks: U.S. Army War College, 07 May 1998), 3; available from http://handle.dtic.mil/100.2/ADA350972; Internet; accessed 13 March 2006.

[30] Gary Felicetti and John Luce, "The Posse Comitatus Act: Liberation from the Lawyers," *Parameters* 34 (Autumn 2004): 98; available from carlisle-www.army.mil/usawc/Parameters/04autumn/felicett.pdf; Internet; accessed 13 March 2006.

[31] Doyle, 10.

[32] Chipman, 5;  1878 Army Appropriations Act (June 18, 1878, ch. 263 § 15, 20 Stat. 152).

[33] Ibid.

[34] *Use of Army and Air Force as Posse Comitatus.*

[35] Mackubin Thomas Owens, "Maintaining the Divide," *National Review Online*, 26 October 2005 [journal on-line]; available from http://www.nationalreview.com/owens/owens200510260824.asp; Internet; accessed 24 January 2006.

[36] Ibid.

[37] Felicetti and Luce, 100.

[38] Ibid.

[39] Ibid.

[40] Toomer, 25.

[41] Ibid., 10; U.S. Department of Defense, *DoD Cooperation with Civilian Law Enforcement Officials*, DoD Directive 5525.5 (Washington, D.C.: U.S. Department of Defense, 15 January 1986), 22; available from http://www.dtic.mil/whs/directives/corres/pdf2/d55255p.pdf; Internet; accessed 26 February 2006; U.S. Department of the Navy, *Cooperation with Civilian Law Enforcement Officials*, SECNAV Instruction 5820.7B (Washington, D.C.: U.S. Department of the Navy, 28 March 1988), 4; available from http://neds.daps.dla.mil/Directives/5820b7.pdf; Internet; accessed 26 February 2006.

[42] Toomer., 25.  While the Coast Guard is organized under the Department of Homeland Security in peacetime, and transferred to the Department of Navy upon declaration of war or when the President directs, the Coast Guard is statutorily authorized to perform law enforcement missions by Title 14 U.S.C. Section 2.

[43] John R. Brinkerhoff, "The Posse Comitatus Act and Homeland Security," *Journal of Homeland Security*, February 2002 [journal on-line]; available from http://www.homelandsecurity.org/journal/Articles/brinkerhoffpossecomitatus.htm; Internet; accessed 19 February 2006; see also *National Guard in Federal Service: Status*, U.S. Code vol. 10, sec. 12405 (1994), available from http://www.law.cornell.edu/uscode/html/uscode10/usc_sec_10_00012405----000-.html; Internet; accessed 02 March 2006.

[44] U.S. Department of Defense, *DoD Cooperation with Civilian Law Enforcement Officials*, DoD Directive 5525.5 (Washington, D.C.: U.S. Department of Defense, 15 January 1986), 6; available from http://www.dtic.mil/whs/directives/corres/pdf2/d55255p.pdf; Internet; accessed 26 February 2006.

[45] Donald J. Currier, *The Posse Comitatus Act: A Harmless Relic from the Post-Reconstruction Era or a Legal Impediment to Transformation?* (Carlisle Barracks: U.S. Army War College, September 2003), 1; available from http://handle.dtic.mil/100.2/ADA417183; Internet; accessed 13 March 2006.

[46] Ibid., 9.

[47] Hammond.

[48] U.S. Constitution, art. 2, sec. 2.

[49] U.S. Constitution, art. 2, sec. 3.

[50] U.S. Constitution, art. 4, sec 4.

[51] Doyle, 14-15.

[52] Ibid., 17-18.

[53] 7 Cong. Rec. 4648 (1878).

[54] Ibid., 15.

[55] *Employment of Military Resources in the Event of Civil Disturbances--Legal Considerations*, Code of Federal Regulations, vol. 32, sec. 215.4(c)(1) (2005). (1) The constitutional exceptions are two in number and are based upon the inherent legal right of the U.S. Government--a sovereign national entity under the Federal Constitution--to insure the preservation of public order and the carrying out of governmental operations within its territorial limits, by force if necessary. (i) The emergency authority. Authorities [sic] prompt and vigorous Federal action, including use of military forces, to prevent loss of life or wanton destruction of property and to restore governmental functioning and public order when sudden and unexpected civil disturbances, disasters, or calamities seriously endanger life and property and disrupt normal governmental functions to such an extent that duly constituted local authorities are unable to control the situations. (ii) Protection of Federal property and functions. Authorizes Federal action, including the use of military forces, to protect Federal property and Federal governmental functions when the need for protection exists and duly constituted local authorities are unable or decline to provide adequate protection.

[56] *Insurrection*, U.S. Code, vol. 10, Chap. 15 (1956). See also first Insurrection Act, 1 Stat. 264 (May 2, 1792). U.S. Code available from http://www.law.cornell.edu/uscode/.

[57] Insurrection, U.S. Code, vol. 10, sec. 331-335 (1956); U.S. Constitution, art. 1, sec. 8.

[58] Employment *of Military Resources in the Event of Civil Disturbances--Legal Considerations*, Code of Federal Regulations, vol. 32, sec. 215.4(c)(2)(i)(a) (2005).  C.F.R. available from http://www.gpoaccess.gov/cfr/index.html.

[59] *Ibid.,* vol. 32, sec. 215.4(c)(2)(i)(b).

[60] *Ibid.,* vol. 32, sec. 215.4(c)(2)(i)(c).

[61] Ibid. , vol. 32, sec. 215.4(c)(2)(i).

[62] *Guam and Virgin Islands included as "State,"* U.S. Code, vol. 10, sec. 335 (1968).

[63] Ibid.

[64] Toomer, 30.

[65] Steven L. Miller, *The Military, Domestic Law Enforcement, and Posse Comitatus: A Time for Change* (Maxwell AFB: Air Command and Staff College, April 2000), 7-10; available from https://research.maxwell.af.mil/viewabstract.aspx?id=2301; Internet; accessed 13 March 2006.

[66] Miller, 7.

[67] *Military Support For Civilian Law Enforcement Agencies*, U.S. Code, vol. 10, chap. 18 (1989); available from http://www.law.cornell.edu/uscode/html/uscode10/usc_sup_01_10_10_A_20_I_30_18.html; Internet; accessed 01 March 2006.

[68] *Restriction on Direct Participation by Military Personnel*, U.S. Code, vol. 10, sec. 375 (1989); available from http://frwebgate.access.gpo.gov/cgi-bin/getdoc.cgi?dbname= browse_usc&docid=Cite:+10USC375; Internet; accessed 01 March 2006.

[69] *Assignment of Coast Guard Personnel to Naval Vessels for Law Enforcement Purposes*, U.S. Code, vol. 10, sec. 379 (1989); available from http://frwebgate.access.gpo.gov/cgi-bin/getdoc.cgi?dbname=browse_usc&docid=Cite:+10USC379; Internet; accessed 04 March 2006.

[70] Ibid., 7-8.

[71] Toomer, 20-21.

[72] Chipman, 8.

[73] *Homeland Security Act of 2002*, PL 107-296, sec. 886 (November 25, 2002). SEC. 886. SENSE OF CONGRESS REAFFIRMING THE CONTINUED IMPORTANCE ANDAPPLICABILITY OF THE POSSE COMITATUS ACT. (a) FINDINGS- Congress finds the following: (1) Section 1385 of title 18, United States Code (commonly known as the `Posse Comitatus Act') prohibits the use of the Armed Forces as a posse comitatus to execute the laws except in cases and under circumstances expressly authorized by the Constitution or Act of Congress.  (2) Enacted in 1878, the Posse Comitatus Act was expressly intended to prevent United States Marshals, on their own initiative, from calling on the Army for assistance in

enforcing Federal law. (3) The Posse Comitatus Act has served the Nation well in limiting the use of the Armed Forces to enforce the law. (4) Nevertheless, by its express terms, the Posse Comitatus Act is not a complete barrier to the use of the Armed Forces for a range of domestic purposes, including law enforcement functions, when the use of the Armed Forces is authorized by Act of Congress or the President determines that the use of the Armed Forces is required to fulfill the President's obligations under the Constitution to respond promptly in time of war, insurrection, or other serious emergency. (5) Existing laws, including chapter 15 of title 10, United States Code (commonly known as the `Insurrection Act'), and the Robert T. Stafford Disaster Relief and Emergency Assistance Act (42 U.S.C. 5121 et seq.), grant the President broad powers that may be invoked in the event of domestic emergencies, including an attack against the Nation using weapons of mass destruction, and these laws specifically authorize the President to use the Armed Forces to help restore public order. (b) SENSE OF CONGRESS-Congress reaffirms the continued importance of section 1385 of title 18, United States Code, and it is the sense of Congress that nothing in this Act should be construed to alter the applicability of such section to any use of the Armed Forces as a posse comitatus to execute the laws.

[74] Currier, 7.

[75] Ibid., 7-8.

[76] Ibid., 8.

[77] Ibid., 17.

[78] Miller, 5.

[79] *Robert T. Stafford Disaster Relief and Emergency Assistance Act*, U.S. Code, vol. 42, sec. 5170b; available from http://www.fema.gov/library/stafact.shtm; Internet; accessed 01 March 2006.

[80] Ibid.

[81] *Robert T. Stafford Disaster Relief and Emergency Assistance Act*, U.S. Code, vol. 42, chap. 68 (2000).

[82] Ibid.

[83] *Employment of Military Resources in the Event of Civil Disturbances--Legal Considerations*, Code of Federal Regulations, vol. 32, sec. 215.4(c).

[84] Doyle, 21-22. List of 24 statutory exceptions to the PCA: 5 U.S.C. App. (Inspector General Act of 1978) 8(g) (Department of Defense Inspector General is not limited by the Posse Comitatus Act (18 U.S.C. 1385) in carrying out audits and investigations under the Act); 10 U.S.C. 331-335 (President may use the militia and armed forces to suppress insurrection and enforce federal authority in the face of rebellion or other forms of domestic violence); 10 U.S.C. 374 note (§1004 of the National Defense Authorization Act for 1991, as amended) (during fiscal years 1991 through 2002, the Secretary of Defense may provide counter-drug activity assistance upon request of federal or state law enforcement agencies); 10 U.S.C. 382 (the Secretary of Defense may provide assistance to the Department of Justice in emergency

situations involving chemical or biological weapons of mass destruction); 10 U.S.C. 382 note (§1023 of the National Defense Authorization Act for Fiscal Year 2000) (during fiscal years 2000 through 2004, the Secretary of Defense may provide assistance to federal and state law enforcement agencies to respond to terrorism or threats of terrorism); 16 U.S.C. 23 (Secretary of the Army may detail troops to protect Yellowstone National Park upon the request of the Secretary of the Interior); 16 U.S.C. 78 (Secretary of the Army may detail troops to protect Sequoia and Yosemite National Parks upon the request of the Secretary of the Interior); 16 U.S.C. 593 (President may use the land and naval forces of the United States to prevent destruction of federal timber in Florida); 16 U.S.C. 1861(a) (Secretary of Transportation (or the Secretary of the Navy in time of war) may entering into agreements for the use of personnel and resources of other federal or state agencies -- including those of the Department of Defense -- for the enforcement of the Magnuson Fishery Conservation and Management Act); 18 U.S.C. 112, 1116 (Attorney General may request the assistance of federal or state agencies -- including the Army, Navy and Air Force -- to protect foreign dignitaries from assault, manslaughter and murder); 18 U.S.C. 351 (FBI may request the assistance of any federal or state agency -- including the Army, Navy and Air Force -- in its investigations of the assassination, kidnapping or assault of a Member of Congress); 18 U.S.C. 831 (Attorney General may request assistance from the Secretary of Defense for enforcement of the proscriptions against criminal transactions in nuclear materials)(18 U.S.C. 175a, 229E, and 2332e cross reference to the Attorney General's authority under 10 U.S.C. 381 to request assistance from the Secretary in an emergency involving biological weapons, chemical weapons, and weapons of mass destruction respective); 18 U.S.C. 1751 (FBI may request the assistance of any federal or state agency – including the Army, Navy and Air Force -- in its investigations of the assassination, kidnapping or assault of the President); 18 U.S.C. 3056 (Director of the Secret Service may request assistance from the Department of Defense and other federal agencies to protect the President); 22 U.S.C. 408 (President may use the land and naval forces of the United States to enforce Title IV of the Espionage Act of 1917 (22 U.S.C. 401-408)); 22 U.S.C. 461 (President may use the land and naval forces and militia of the United States to seize or detain ships used in violation of the Neutrality Act); 22 U.S.C. 462 (President may use the land and naval forces and militia of the United States to detain or compel departure of foreign ships under the provisions of the Neutrality Act); 25 U.S.C. 180 (President may use military force to remove trespassers from Indian treaty lands); 42 U.S.C. 98 (Secretary of the Navy at the request of the Public Health Service may make vessels or hulks available to quarantine authority at various U.S. ports); 42 U.S.C. 1989 (magistrates issuing arrest warrants for civil rights violations may authorize those serving the warrants to call for assistance from bystanders, the posse comitatus, or the land or naval forces or militia of the United States; 42 U.S.C. 5170b (Governor of state in which a major disaster has occurred may request the President to direct the Secretary of Defense to permit the use of DoD personnel for emergency work necessary for the preservation of life and property); 43 U.S.C. 1065 (President may use military force to remove unlawful enclosures from the public lands); 48 U.S.C. 1418 (President may use the land and naval forces of the United States to protect the rights of owners in guano islands); 48 U.S.C. 1422 (Governor of Guam may request assistance of senior military or naval commander of the armed forces of the United States in cases of disaster, invasion, insurrection, rebellion or imminent danger thereof, or of lawless violence); 48 U.S.C. 1591 (Governor of the Virgin Islands may request assistance of senior military or naval commander of the armed forces of the United States in the Virgin Islands or Puerto Rico in cases of disaster, invasion, insurrection, rebellion or imminent danger thereof, or of lawless violence); 50 U.S.C. 220 (President may use the Army, Navy or militia to prevent the unlawful removal of vessels or cargoes from customs areas during times of insurrection).

[85] *Uniting and Strengthening America by Providing Appropriate Tools Required to Intercept and Obstruct Terrorism (USA PATRIOT ACT) Act of 2001: Requests for Military Assistance to Enforce Prohibition in Certain Emergencies*, P.L. 107-56, sec. 104 (2001).

[86] Province, 52.

[87] Edward P. Richards, III, "Martial Law," available from http://biotech.law.lsu.edu/cases/nat-sec/martial-law.htm; Internet; accessed 04 March 2006.

[88] Ibid.

[89] *Constitutional Topic: Martial Law*, available from http://www.usconstitution.net/consttop_mlaw.html; Internet; accessed 04 March 2006.

[90] Ibid.; E*x parte Milligan*, 71 US 2 (1866).

[91] Ibid.

[92] Ibid.; *Martial Law*, Code of Federal Regulations, vol. 32 sec 501.4 (2005).

[93] Ibid.

[94] Richards.

[95] U.S. Joints Chiefs of Staff, *Homeland Security*, Joint Publication 3-26 (Washington, D.C.: U.S. Joint Chiefs of Staff, 02 August 2005); available from www.dtic.mil/doctrine/jel/new_pubs/jp3_26.pdf; Internet; accessed 13 March 2006. JP-36 divides the military mission into Homeland Defense and Civil Support (CS). Employment of military forces within the US, its territories, and possessions provided under the auspices of CS, typically falls under the broad mission of Military Assistance to Civil Authorities (MACA). MACA operations consist of three subordinate missions. They may overlap and DOD may, depending on the circumstances, provide support to them simultaneously. They are military support to civil authorities (MSCA), military support to civil law enforcement agencies (MSCLEA), and military assistance for civil disturbances (MACDIS). MSCA missions respond to natural disasters, special events, and manmade disasters. MSCLEA missions are counterterrorism, national special security event support, counterdrug, maritime security, and loans of equipment, facilities, or personnel. MACDIS missions respond to insurrections, riots, or to assist in maintaining law and order.

[96] The respective service publications, especially SECNAVINST 5820.7B , Cooperation with Civilian Law Enforcement Officials, 1988; and AR 500-51, Support to Civilian Law Enforcement Agencies, 1983 are also outdated and poorly written. AFI 10-801, Assistance to Civilian Law Enforcement Agencies, 1994 and AFI 10-802, Military Support to Civilian Authorities, 2002 are more current and appropriately written.

[97] Need reference location of extent practical and maximum extent practicable

[98] JP 3-26, IV-12.

[99] U.S. Constitution, preamble.

[100] Congressional Research Service, The Library of Congress, "Hurricane Katrina - Stafford Act Authorities and Actions by Governor Blanco and President Bush to Trigger Them," memorandum for the Honorable John Conyers, Jr., Washington, D.C.,12 September 2005; available from http://www.au.af.mil/au/awc/awcgate/crs/12sep05memo.pdf; Internet; accessed 12 March 2006.  The President also signed the disaster declaration immediately after or possibly as Hurricane Katrina made landfall on 29 August 2005.

[101] Francis Fragos Townsend, *The Federal Response to Hurricane Katrina: Lessons Learned* (Washington, D.C.: The White House, February 2006), 37; available from http://www.whitehouse.gov/reports/katrina-lessons-learned.pdf; Internet; accessed 12 March 2006.

[102] Evan Thomas, "How Bush Blew It: Bureaucratic Timidity. Bad Phone Lines. And a Failure of Imagination. Why the Government Was So Slow to Respond to Catastrophe," *Newsweek*, 19 September 2005 [magazine on-line]; available from http://www.msnbc.msn.com/id/9287434/site/newsweek/; Internet; accessed 23 January 2006.

[103] Steve Bowman, Lawrence Kapp, and Amy Belasco, *Hurricane Katrina: DOD Disaster Response* (Washington, D.C.: Congressional Research Service, The Library of Congress, 19 September 2005), 11; available from http://www.fas.org/sgp/crs/natsec/RL33095.pdf; Internet; accessed 12 March 2006.

[104] Thomas.

[105] Ibid.

[106] Manual Roig-Franzia and Spencer Hsu, "Many Evacuated, but Thousands Still Waiting," *Washington Post*, 04 September 2005 [newspaper on-line]; available from http://www.washingtonpost.com/wp-dyn/content/article/2005/09/03/AR2005090301680.html; Internet; accessed 23 January 2006.

[107] Eric Lipton, Eric Schmitt, and Thom Shanker, "Political Issues Snarled Plans for Troop Aid," *New York Times*, 08 September 2005 [newspaper on-line]; available from http://www.nytimes.com/2005/09/09/national/nationalspecial/09military.html?ex=1283918400&en=aa642c95881a7c01&ei=5089&partner=rssyahoo&emc=rss; Internet; accessed 20 January 2006.

[108] JP 3-26, IV-1.

[109] Bowman, Kapp, and Belasco, 6.

[110] Ibid., 3,11.

[111] Townsend, 43.

[112] Ibid.

[113] Scott Shane and Thom Shanker, "When Storm Hit, National Guard Was Deluged Too," *New York Times*, 28 September 2005 [newspaper on-line]; available from

http://leahy.senate.gov/press/200509/092905b.html#NYT1; Internet; accessed 20 January 2006.

[114] Ibid.

[115] "Martial Law Clarified," *Times-Picayune,"* 30 August 2005 [newspaper on-line]; available from http://www.nola.com/weblogs/print.ssf?/mtlogs/nola_Times-Picayune/archives/print075262.html; Internet; accessed 23 January 2006.

[116] "Nagin Declares Martial Law to Crack Down on Looters," *WWL TV*, 31 August 2005 [newspaper on-line]; available from http://www.wwltv.com/local/stories/WWL083105lawless.1242410b.html; Internet; accessed 23 January 2006.

[117] Alex Berenson and Sewell Chan, "Forced Evacuation of a Battered New Orleans Begins," *New York Times*, 07 September 2005 [newspaper on-line]; available from http://www.globalaging.org/elderrights/us/2005/evacuation.htm; Internet; accessed 20 January 2006.

[118] Keelin McDonell,"What Is Martial Law?: And Is New Orleans Under It?," *Slate*, 02 September 2005 [newspaper on-line]; available from http://www.slate.com/id/2125584/; Internet; accessed 23 January 2006.

[119] Ibid.

[120] Richards.

[121] Bill Sammon, "Bush Offers Pentagon as 'Lead Agency' in Disasters," *The Washington Times*, 26 September 2005 [newspaper on-line]; available from http://www.washtimes.com/national/20050926-122858-7624r.htm; Internet; accessed 13 March 2006.

[122] Townsend, 43.

[123] Repeal of the PCA alone would not allow for the military to accomplish the entire range of the law enforcement mission given the many additional statutory and policy restrictions. For example, Title 10 Section 375 would still apply in prohibiting search, seizure, arrest, or other similar activity while accomplishing actions under Title 10 Chapter 8. See discussion on DoD Directives for example of restrictions established by policy.

[124] Currier, 15-16.

[125] Toomer, 15-16.

[126] Vernon Loeb, "Review of Military's Domestic Role Urged," *Washington Post*, 05 October 2001 [newspaper on-line]; available from http://www.washingtonpost.com/ac2/wp-dyn?pagename=article&contentId=A8944-2001Oct4&notFound=true; Internet; accessed 25 February 2006.

[127] Idid.

[128] U.S. Congress, Senate, Committee on Armed Services, *Committee on Armed Services Hearing on the Role of the Department of Defense in Homeland Security*, 107th Cong., 1st sess., 25 October 2001, opening statement of Senator Levin; available from http://www.senate.gov/~levin/newsroom/release.cfm?id=211580; Internet; accessed 26 February 2006.

[129] Chipman, 2.

[130] Currier, 15.

[131] Toomer, 15; Currier, 15.

[132] Chipman, 8.

[133] Ibid.

[134] Toomer, 30.

[135] Ibid.

[136] Ibid., 1.

[137] Ibid.

[138] Ibid., 17.

[139] Ibid.

[140] Ibid., 24.

[141] Currier, 16.

[142] Toomer, 16.

[143] Ibid.

[144] Ibid.

[145] Ibid., 33.

[146] SGT Sara Wood, USA, "DoD Leaders Report on Hurricane Response," American Forces Press Service, 10 November 2005 [newspaper on-line]; available from http://www.defenselink.mil/news/Nov2005/20051110_3310.html; Internet; accessed 08 December 2005.

[147] Chipman, 17-18.

[148] Alan Bock, "Posse Comitatus: Remembering Why," 01 October 2005; available from http://www.antiwar.com/bock/?articleid=7468; Internet; access 08 December 2005.

[149] Chipman, 7.

[150] Bock.

[151] Hammond.

[152] Ibid.

[153] Chipman, 7.

[154] Toomer, 31-32.

[155] David Isenberg, "Posse Comitatus: Caution Is Necessary," Center for Defense Information, 06 August 2002; available from http://www.cdi.org/terrorism/pcomitatus-pr.cfm; Internet; accessed 08 December 2005.

[156] Hammond.

[157] Isenberg.

[158] Ibid.

[159] Ibid., 16.

[160] Toomer, 31-32.

[161] Bock.

[162] Toomer, 32.

[163] Bock.

[164] MAJ Craig T. Trebilcock, USAR, "The Myth of Posse Comitatus," October 2000; available from http://www.homelandsecurity.org/journal/articles/Trebilcock.htm; Internet; accessed 08 December 2005.

[165] Isenberg.

[166] Miller, 16-17.

[167] Trebilcock.

[168] Toomer, 33.

[169] Quote from Yogi Berra, available from http://www.yogiberra.com/yogi-isms.html; Internet; accessed 08 December 2005.

[170] Chipman, 15.

[171] Toomer, 15.

[172] Ibid.

[173] Hammond.

[174] Ibid.

[175] Ibid.

[176] Ibid.

[177] Toomer, 33.

[178] Department of the Navy and Army corresponding instructions and regulations are outdated, while the Department of the Air Force instruction is current, they all contain the misquoted PCA including the $10,000 fine.

[179] Currier, 15.

[180] Ibid.

[181] Chipman, 2.

[182] Currier, 15.